Raising
Godly Kids

THIS BOOK IS A SPECIAL GIFT

FROM

___

TO

___

DATE

___

Raising
Godly Kids

STELLA AMARACHI NWOKENKWO

ISBN: 978-3-00-073274-4

Independently Published.

Unless otherwise stated, all scriptures are taken from the New International Version (NIV) of the Holy Bible.

DEDICATION

This book is dedicated to my family and to every parent who wants to raise godly seeds for the Lord.

Table of Contents

Introduction **11**

1 Understanding Our Place as Godly Parents **13**

2 Partnering with The Holy Spirit in Your Parenting Journey **19**

3 Responsibilities of a Godly Parent **27**

4 What Do Children Represent **37**

5 Maintaining an Altar of Prayer as Parents **49**

6 Faith and Solid Foundation in Christ **55**

7 Discipleship with Our Children **61**

8 Training the Children to Serve God and Humanity **69**

9 Parental Lessons **77**

A Quick Check-Up for Every Godly Parent **81**

Acknowledgements **83**

Introduction

As parents, our first duty is to have a relationship with the giver of godly seeds—that's our heavenly Father. We cannot have a relationship with Him if we do not know His Word, and the Word of God is the Bible (the divine manual) which helps us to understand our spiritual assignment because our job description is well explained in it.

Having a relationship with the Father leads us to maintain a loving relationship with the Holy Spirit—our helper—and makes us crave his gifts. As our helper, the Holy Spirit helps us to supervise our parenting journey as long as Jesus tarries.

Raising Godly Kids will help parents understand their parenting responsibility and see it as a spiritual assignment. This book contains some detailed strategies that are necessary to raise Godly children.

1

Understanding Our Place As Godly Parents

Our relationship and fear of the Lord is the secret to receiving divine instructions, wisdom, and understanding of how to handle situations in our parenting journey.

As a godly parent, salvation is the pathway to your relationship with Christ. Proverb 9:10 says:

> *The fear of the LORD is the beginning of wisdom, and knowledge of the Holy One is understanding.*

As a believer, parenting is a spiritual and earthly responsibility given to you by the Lord to care for, train, protect and guide someone. Genesis 1:28 is an indication of this.

A parent is not only the father or mother of a child. Biological parents aside, others take on the role of parenting children when the biological parents or one of them is absent. They include stepparents, legal parents, grandparents, single parents, foster parents and more.

Job 28:23 says:

> *God understands the way to it and he alone knows where it dwells.*

Parenting can be burdensome but when we walk with the Lord, He takes over the burden. Apostle Peter encourages us in 1 Peter 5:7 to:

> *Cast all your anxiety on him (*Jesus*) because he cares for you (*for us*).*

In life, we are saddled with different types of burdens. And parenting is one of them because of the responsibility we are tasked with. We do not need to keep our parenting burdens to ourselves. Instead, let's lay them at the feet of Jesus because He is in a parenting partnership with us.

There is no formula to raising a child but God holds the manual as to how we ought to raise every child here on earth.

Your close relationship gives you access to secrets, divine instructions, wisdom, and understanding from the Manual (Bible)—even the answer to all your questions concerning a particular child can be found in it.

Have you ever thought about the instructions that were given to Noah to build an Ark? God was so detailed in His instruction about the length, width, height, and other things in Genesis 6:15-22.

Noah had a relationship with God. Notwithstanding, he didn't just rely on praying or waiting on God to come down and build the Ark! No, he mobilised his family and certainly, he would have sought knowledge or he was skilled on how to build an Ark.

As a parent, you don't just receive instructions and relax with them. Rather, you wage war in prayers, boost your faith to run with such divine instructions, and also seek knowledge from materials that will aid the manifestation of running with such instructions.

While doing these, don't forget to guard your heart with the holy scripture. Put it into action by training and building your children in line with the instruction you have received from God. Isaiah 54:13 says:

> *All your children will be taught by the Lord, and great will be their peace.*

To raise godly children, we must be godly parents. Who is a godly parent?

- A godly parent fears the Lord and walks in His ways (Psalm 128 vs 1-6).

- A godly parent understands that the family as an institution is ordained by God and stands as a structure for society.
- A godly parent works towards not provoking his children to wrath (Ephesians 6:4).
- A godly parent intentionally, with hard work, trains up his child in the way of the Lord (Proverbs 22:6).
- A godly parent willingly teaches and directs godly instructions to her children everywhere they are (Deuteronomy 11:19).
- A godly parent understands that children are like arrows in the hand of a mighty man, (Psalm 127:3-5) and understands the functions of an arrow in his hand because he is the mighty man.
- A godly parent is one in whose home, Jesus is welcomed, and love and safety reign (Revelations 3:20, Proverbs 18:10).
- A godly parent understands that her parenting responsibility is a spiritual task and is ready to be used as a vessel for this purpose to glorify God.
- A godly parent stands in the gap prayerfully for her family, forms a hedge of fire and refuses to let loose the spiritual security of her household for the enemy to creep in (Psalm 34:7).
- A godly parent meditates on God's words to successfully carry out his responsibility as a

parent. The Bible is your manual for good profiting (1 Timothy 4:15, Joshua 1:8).

- A godly parent forbids not his children to come unto Jesus but corrects his children. (Proverbs 13:24, 29:17, Matthew 19:14).
- A godly parent can be likened to an eagle who watches over her eggs before they are hatched and trains them to fly.
- A godly parent is one whose house activities glorify God (Isaiah 32:18).
- A godly parent testifies about the good works of Jesus and the prophetic power of God to his children.
- A godly parent seeks divine wisdom from God. The ostrich in Job 39:13-19 was deprived of wisdom.
- A godly parent is willing to work with the Holy Spirit, the instructor and helper who teaches all things. (1 Cor 2:10, John 14:26).
- A godly parent intentionally works toward raising good seeds (children) for the kingdom of God than raising seeds (children) for the wicked ones (Matthew 13:38).
- A godly parent teaches his children not to consent to ungodly acts (Proverbs 1:10).
- A godly parent exposes his children to understand the mysteries of the kingdom of heaven (Matthew 13:8).

- A godly parent is his children's first pastor (shepherd); he yields to God's instructions (Jeremiah 3:15). God promised your children a shepherd even before their existence.
- A godly parent understands the need for his children to meditate and store God's word in their hearts, instead of depending on human storage devices that may fail them (Proverbs 2:1, Psalm 119:11, Joshua 1:8).

2

Partnering With The Holy Spirit In Your Parenting Journey

Being a Godly parent requires us to be filled and led by the Holy Spirit. When we understand the works of the Holy Spirit as parents, it makes our parenting easier and panic-free especially when things don't go as planned.

In John 16:7–8, Christ told his followers that:

> *But very truly I tell you, it is for your good that I am going away. Unless I go away, the* ***Advocate*** *will not come to you; but if I go, I will send him to you. When he comes, he will prove the world to be in the wrong about sin and righteousness and judgment:*

The Advocate in the scripture above is the Holy Spirit. With this, we can say the Holy Spirit is God's presence inhabited in man.

As a godly parent, your work with the Holy Spirit will not only expose deep revelations about parenting, you may develop the need for the gifts of the Holy Spirit to function gloriously.

Here are some of the ways that the Holy Spirit impacts our parenting.

1. The Holy Spirit Teaches Us All Things Including Godly Parenting: Through the power of the Holy Spirit, we understand the divine manual for godly parenting. There is no parenting manual for children in any age group —0 to Toddlers, Pre-Teenagers and Teenagers—none at all. At each stage of their lives, parents are faced with some parenting difficulties. Involving the Holy Spirit in our daily parenting makes life easier because He gives wisdom, counsel, and divine idea or direction to dealing with every situation we are faced with. We should trust Him.

1 Cor 2:10 (KJV) says:

> *But God hath revealed them unto us by his Spirit: for the Spirit searches all things, yea, the deep things of God.*

John 14:26 also says that:

> *But the Advocate, the Holy Spirit, whom the Father will send in my name, will teach you all things and will remind you of everything I have said to you.*

Through the help of the Holy Spirit, you can multi-function as your children's pastor, school teacher, chef, sports instructor etc. You can also outsource some functions when you need to.

2. The Holy Spirit Intercedes For Us Over Fear Or Challenge About Our Children: As godly parents, we need not be ignorant of the devices of the enemy. At the same time, we need to guard our hearts.

Eph 6:12 (KJV) makes us understand that:

> *For we wrestle not against flesh and blood, but against principalities, against powers, against the rulers of the darkness of this world, against spiritual wickedness in high places.*

Challenges we encounter in parenting can come in the form of sickness, a disobedient spirit being displayed in our children's life, signs of the fruit of the flesh that may lead them to destruction, or even fear of the unknown. As our comforter, we can rely on the Holy Spirit. He makes intercessions for us which cannot be uttered (Romans 8:26).

Prayers do wonders and every parent needs to stand in the gap praying for their children and their children's future.

3. The Holy Spirit Reveals To Us What Is Yet To Come Or Happen: As godly parents, we must embrace the knowledge that the deep things belong to God and He reveals them through His Spirit that is at work in us. Deuteronomy 29:29 says:

> *The secret things belong to the Lord our God, but the things revealed belong to us and to our children forever.*

The Holy Spirit reveals to us great things that are yet to happen in the lives of our children. He also reveals the plot of the enemy and gives us insight into how to deal with it. Still, He remains standing in the gap of prayers for us.

As a godly parent, document the revelations you get concerning your children. Most of the things that have happened in my life today, when I share the details with my mother, she usually brings out her journal and tells me the date and where she was when the Holy Spirit revealed that to her. Sometimes, when I'd been faced with certain challenges, her calls or visits helped me to avert the plans of the enemy.

The actions taken differ from one parent to another. What is common is the fact that the Holy Spirit reveals things to us and how we act on those revelations is important. For me, when I feel the urge to pray for my kids, I do it deliberately and immediately. You must not know why you have to pray, just pray. Also, pray in the holy ghost if you can.

4. The Spirit Guides Every Godly Parent To All Truth (John 16:13): As a godly parent, it is the Spirit of God at work in your life that opens you up to the truth. It varies in different aspects of life, from decision-making for your children to raising them to glorify God.

When we choose activities for the social life of our children and the kind of association they are exposed to, the Holy Spirit guides us to make the right decisions for them. He helps us to adopt a good moral standard that will portray Jesus Christ because we are expected to raise children in whose life His image will reflect for others to emulate.

The Holy Spirit also reveals the truth or gives us clues as to which direction to mould a particular child for what God intends for the child.

As a godly parent, embrace the truth from God's word. This will give room for the Holy Spirit to aid you in your parenting journey because He teaches all things.

1 John 2:20 (AMP) says:

But you have an anointing from the Holy One [you have been set apart, specially gifted and prepared by the Holy Spirit], and all of you know [the truth because He teaches us, illuminates our minds, and guards us against error].

Parenting In The Fruit Of The Spirit, Not Acts Of The Flesh

As parents, when your spirit is joyful or experiencing the fruit of the Holy Spirit, your emotional environment is spiritually sanitised and it extends to your children, your spouse, and those around you.

Galatians 5:22-26 talks about the fruits of the Spirit:

But the fruit of the Spirit is love, joy, peace, forbearance, kindness, goodness, faithfulness, 23 gentlenesses, and self-control. Against such things, there is no law. 24 Those who belong to Christ Jesus have crucified the flesh with its passions and desires. 25 Since we live by the Spirit, let us keep in step with the Spirit. 26 Let us not become conceited, provoking, and envying each other.

Backtracking, we see that the opposite of the fruit of the Spirit is borne out of the acts of the flesh. Galatians 5:19-21 (AMP) talks about this:

> *Now the practices of the sinful nature are clearly evident: they are sexual immorality, impurity, sensuality (total irresponsibility, lack of self-control), idolatry, sorcery, hostility, strife, jealousy, fits of* ***anger, disputes****, dissensions, factions [that promote heresies], envy, drunkenness, riotous behavior, and other things like these. I warn you beforehand, just as I did previously, that those who practice such things will not inherit the kingdom of God.*

Let's focus on Disputes, Anger or Malice as fruits of the flesh. Most parents have directly or indirectly transferred anger, disputes, and malice to their children. When parents get into a dispute with someone or a family member and choose to quarrel with that person, they give their children reasons to follow suit. Some parents, at times, even explain to their children an attitude to portray when they see such a person.

The Bible says that whoever practices such behaviour will not inherit heaven. We must account for our actions on judgment day.

Mark 9:42 (AMP) tells us that:

> *Whoever causes one of these little ones who believe and trust in Me to stumble [that is, to sin or lose faith], it would be better for him if a heavy millstone [one requiring a donkey's strength to*

turn it] were hung around his neck and he were thrown into the sea.

The above scripture is clear. As shepherds, trusted with the responsibility of raising our children, we must not lead them down the wrong path. No matter your weakness, God is always willing to fill you with grace to stand strong. Acknowledge those areas, deliberately work towards them and see yourself triumphing gloriously. In your struggling parenting heart, embrace the fruit of the Holy Spirit and consciously grow in the word of God for a better living.

Works Of The Fruit Of The Flesh

- It takes away your peace
- It steals your joy
- It contends with your salvation
- It makes you disconnect spiritually if not addressed
- It can lead to destruction
- It can slow your breakthroughs' and blessings.

3

Responsibilities Of A Godly Parent

In the same way that an employee is given responsibilities when employed, we also have been given responsibilities to help us parent the children God has given us.

Let's look at some of these responsibilities.

It Is Our Duty To Wear The Garment Of Salvation As A Parent

Godly parenting requires us first to wear the garment of salvation to fully be invited to enjoy the divine secrets in our parenting journey (Isaiah 61:10). As godly parents, the garment of salvation gives us access to the banquet with the King of kings (Matthew 22:1-14). The garment of salvation gives us access to unique spiritual foods, and ideas to function without boundaries as His divine strength and grace are always available to help us work out our salvation.

I pray that every godly parent will receive grace to wear this garment of salvation to be able to access the banquet with the Lord on that wedding day when we shall meet our bridegroom.

It Is Our Duty To Model Christ To Our Children

Making Jesus Christ the role model for your children is extremely important, and the good news is that such is achievable through the following:

- Christlike living
- Spoken words and actions
- Relationship with family, friends, and the public
- Heart of commitment, fear, and love for God
- Modest appearance in every ramification
- Hospitality and your counsel
- Nature of fun that pleases God you partake in
- Spiritual activities you practice before them

It Is Our Duty To Be Our Children's First Pastor Here On Earth

As a godly parent, remember that in Jeremiah 3:15, God promised our children before their existence that He will give them pastors (shepherds) according to His heart, which shall feed them with knowledge and understanding. Dear parent, you are that pastor!

Children have many needs—physical, emotional, spiritual, etc. As a godly parent, you need divine wisdom, which is profitable to direct, and help from above to meet up to these needs.

Endeavour not to shift your responsibility to the school, church, or circular teachers, because they are only there to support you.

Deuteronomy 6:6-7 says:

> *These commandments that I give you today are to be on your hearts. Impress them on your children. Talk about them when you sit at home and when you walk along the road, when you lie down and when you get up.*

Carefully pay attention to these:

- When you are seated in the house
- While on the way
- Before you lie down at night
- When you rise in the morning

Every parent needs divine insights and grace to be their children's first pastor on earth, to lead and also to finish well.

It Is Our Duty To Parent In Boldness, Not Fear

Among all the great responsibilities God instructed man to do, such as taking care of the animals and the earth, He also instructed us to care for and raise children in the way of the Lord. As parents, we know that things happen and unplanned or unexpected situations surface in our parenting journey. Nevertheless, we must be encouraged in the Lord not to lose our boldness to fear in parenting our children.

Fear gives room to the enemy to break some values we have built in our children. According to 2 Timothy 1:7, God has not given us a spirit of fear but of power and love and discipline.

If you have lost boldness to fear on this parenting journey, you can return to the Creator who knows the beginning from the end, and who can also recreate your story. The way He recreated the story of Jabez.

In my earliest parenting journey, the fear of having what it takes to raise a godly child almost burdened me. There was no better way for me to overcome it than soaking myself in God's promises and listening to other godly parents share their testimonies.

As parents, when we find ourselves losing our boldness, the altar of prayer where we communicate with God who has the divine manual for godly parenting is of utmost importance. By praying the promises of God's word from the Bible, we regain our confidence.

Ephesians 3:12 (AMP) says:

> *In whom we have boldness and confident access through faith in Him [that is, our faith gives us sufficient courage to freely and openly approach God through Christ].*

BE BOLD!!

It Is Our Duty To Parent In Love

Dear parent, knowing what correction is good or beneficial for your children and not enforcing them because you don't want to hurt their feelings or make them angry at you is not parenting in love but fear. Parenting in love does not mean we should abuse our children. When we understand that they are God's heritage, we will correct them constructively and not criticise them destructively. We will also correct and lead them by our good example.

We read in 1 Peter 5:3 (NLT) that:

> *Don't lord it over the people assigned to your care, but lead them by your own good example.*

The question is, how well are you modelling Christlike life to your children? As godly parents, we need to keep working out our salvation to enable us to live Christlike. Most of the time, when dealing with pre-teenagers and teenagers, fear creeps in when considering what disciplinary measure to apply.

Proverbs 23:14 gives us an idea about how to discipline.

> *Thou shalt beat him with the rod, and shalt deliver his soul from hell.*

The rod is a symbol of authority that guides and directs and was used in different places in the Bible.

Discipline is like putting pressure on the child you love to redirect his steps. In your discipline, let love lead. Give reasons for such corrections and avoid provoking your children.

Ephesians 6:4 (KJV) tells us:

> *... provoke not your children to wrath but bring them up in the admonition and nurture of the Lord.*

Let our children know that love is the greatest gift of all. Teach them God's kind of love as recorded in 1 Corinthians 13. Depending on the age bracket of your children, devise a means to explain to them the nature of divine love in the scripture. Love is a gift given by the Holy Spirit which He also shares in our hearts (Romans 5:5).

God's desire is for us to share his love with the world. May God help us overcome any fruit of the flesh posing against the gift of love in our children. Amen.

To parent in love:

- Teach them through the written word of God... 1 John 4:8
- Teach them with godly pictures and video stories
- Teach them by living a Christlike lifestyle of love they can emulate
- Teach them the various ways they can practically express divine love through their actions, their hospitality, their material possessions, their spoken words, their character, and also their heart of love towards God and many others.

It Is Our Duty To Hunger For Divine Wisdom In Our Parenting

As godly parents, we either choose to be like an ostrich or an eagle in our parenting. Job 39:13-19 tells us of how an ostrich was deprived of wisdom. She lays her eggs and ignores them but an eagle lays her eggs and watches over them before they are hatched and trains her eaglets to fly.

Be committed to training your children to be able to fly in this evil time. Many things are contending for their attention but remember God said in Isaiah 49:25 that He will contend with those that contend with us.

The family is the first place where children are shaped in preparation for what awaits them in the future. The family as an institution ordained by God stands as a structure for society.

Divine wisdom teaches us to buy the truth to keep the oil in the lives of our children burning. Godly parenting requires divine wisdom like the five wise virgins in Matthew 25:1-13. As godly parents, we are on a divine journey to nurturing godly seeds till our bridegroom comes. While Jesus (The bridegroom) tarries, endeavour to buy the truth (oil) to keep the light burning in the lives of your children. When the day of the bridegroom comes, only the truth shall set them free.

Proverbs 23:23 (KJV) says:

> *Buy the truth, and sell it not; also, wisdom, and instruction, and understanding.*

John 8:32 (KJV) says:

> *And ye shall know the truth, and the truth shall make you free.*

John 10:27-28 says:

> *My sheep hear my voice, and I know them, and they follow me: And I give unto them eternal life, and they shall never perish, neither shall any man pluck them out of my hand.*

May God grant us the wisdom and vision of an eagle who sees far and prepares her children ahead of time.

It Is Our Duty To Be Sensitive To Times And Seasons In Our Parenting

Godly parenting requires us to be sensitive and apply wisdom to times and seasons in our parenting responsibility. Knowing that we are on a spiritual assignment, God's word is the tool we need throughout our parenting. At different stages and phases of our parenting, we need the leading of the Holy Spirit to finish well.

Parents with children of different age groups cannot apply the same method to raise their children—and this applies to spiritual parenting as well. The word of God is the only common tool at all stages. The Holy Spirit will inspire and speak to your spirit the instruction or divine wisdom which you need during the different stages of their lives.

We always have the help of the Holy Spirit except when we disconnect from the flow of spiritual current and seek the way that pleases us.

Philippians 1:6 (AMP) tells us that He will bring to a finality that which He started:

> *I am convinced and confident of this very thing, that He who has begun a good work in you will [continue to] perfect and complete it until the day of Christ Jesus [the time of His return].*

Why does He even bother with us? Hear what Ephesians 2:10 (AMP) says about that:

> *For we are His workmanship [His own masterwork, a work of art], created in Christ Jesus [reborn from above—spiritually transformed, renewed, ready to be used] for good works, which God prepared [for us] beforehand [taking paths which He set] so that we would walk in them [living the good life which He prearranged and made ready for us].*

That scripture makes me feel so precious that I am committed to doing the works that God prepared beforehand.

4

What Do Children Represent

Beyond being our children, our children play different roles or represent different things in our lives. Are you familiar with what children represent?

Children Represent Arrows

Psalm 127: 4 says:

> *As arrows are in the hand of a mighty man; so are children of the youth*

According to the Bible, your children are arrows in your hands and you ought to be careful about how you use them. Abusing this arrow may allow the devil to have victory over you. What do I mean? Don't use your children as tools for revenge on humans. Don't teach your children to lie, hate or talk down on people. If you are experiencing a broken relationship, don't use your child as an arrow to get back at your spouse. If you are a step-parent, don't make your stepchild feel broken.

Generally, in all our dealings with children, we must be cautious of the fact that they are arrows in the hand of the mighty one. We must be willing to keep them spiritually sharp, not blunt, in case the enemy raises its ugly head.

Arrows don't release themselves. They need help to be sharpened and a trigger to make them function. As a parent, you are the trainer described in Proverbs 22:6 (KJV) who should:

> *Train up a child in the way he should go: and when he is old, he will not depart from it.*

Among all tools you may need for this training, the Bible is your divine manual.

If children are arrows in our hands, for the time being, we control their direction and we can help them to stay focused on the target. This is where discipline is used in redirecting their steps.

Proverbs 13:24 (KJV) says:

> *He that spares his rod hates his son: but he that loveth him chastened him.*

When disciplining, have Ephesians 6:4 (KJV) in mind.:

> *And, ye fathers, provoke not your children to wrath: but bring them up in the nurture and admonition of the Lord.*

Focusing Your Arrow (Children)

As godly parents, there is no exact time to carry out these spiritual exercises. Before conception or from the womb, begin to speak the word of God into the lives of your children. Also, play and sing spiritual psalms and songs around them. Scientists have shown that the human fetus can hear and understand vibrations going on outside the mother's body. So, speak and pray into their lives.

Romans 4:17 makes us understand that with our words, we speak out those things which be not (not yet in existence) as though they were by faith because we know that the spiritual controls the physical.

We saw this play out in Luke 1:41 when Mary visited Elisabeth. The Bible tells us that when Elisabeth heard the salutation of Mary, the baby in her womb leapt and Elisabeth was filled with the Holy Spirit.

The word of God is important and powerful:

- Use the word of God as a two-edged sword
- Choose your words carefully as they are a powerful tool.

- Allow the fruit of the Spirit to fill you in your moulding process.

Children Represent Gifts And Seeds

As humans living by God's grace, there are certain gifts we do not deserve but God being a merciful Father freely gives children to us as gifts.

Children are seeds and God expects us, the gardeners, to help Him, the Owner, nurture them to grow. God freely gave us His children as gifts.

James 1:17-18 says:

> *Every good and perfect gift is from above, coming down from the Father of the heavenly lights, who does not change like shifting shadows. He chose to give us birth through the word of truth, that we might be a kind of firstfruits of all he created.*

Think about it, is there a time in your past that you made mistakes, or used certain verbal words or carried out certain actions on a child and you told yourself, "No way, I do not deserve kids!"

A lot of us have been in this place but God says everyone deserves children; they are gifts that He doesn't take back once given.

Roman 11:29 says:

for God's gifts and his call are irrevocable.

Seeds are meant to grow and reproduce after their kind according to the Lord's blessings in Genesis 1. The planting of the seed depends on the farmer (Jesus) not the soil (womb). Only the farmer understands the times and seasons that are good for all seeds. Sometimes a seed might sprout but the farmer from experience may uproot it because he sees challenges that the seed may face that might hinder its growth. Other times, He allows some seeds to face challenges but like the farmer, He is always there to water and nurtures the seeds for strength.

Children Represent Jesus

Jesus said in Mark 9:37:

Whoever welcomes one of these little children in my name welcomes me, and whoever welcomes me does not welcome me but the one who sent me.

Children represent Jesus as seen in the scripture above because of those qualities they easily exhibit—unconditional love, joy with a pure heart, innocence and not being hurtful. God wants us to be like little children and receive Jesus if we must make His kingdom.

And in Matthew 18:10, we read:

> *See that you do not despise one of these little ones. For I tell you that their angels in heaven always see the face of my Father in heaven.*

With the above scriptures, there are no conditions attached to welcoming children. As a parent, the circumstances surrounding your child's birth should not take away the joy of welcoming your baby. By welcoming your child, you welcome Jesus into your home. Welcome children because they are spiritual beings and the spirit of Jesus dwells in them.

Children Represent Heritage And Vessels For Kingdom Growth

Children are the heritage of the Lord because they are future instruments in a process that God will use to proclaim His kingdom here on earth.

The history and message of JESUS are of great importance, that is why He blesses the womb to reproduce and bring forth vessels for the Masters' use.

Psalm 127:3 (KJV) says:

> *Lo children are a heritage from the Lord, the fruit of the womb a reward.*

As parents, you are a steward/caretaker and have been given the opportunity of the fruit of the womb. When this precious fruit is birthed, parents should earnestly seek and desire the gifts of the Holy Spirit (discernment of the spirit, wisdom, faith etc. — 1 Cor 12:8-11) to be able to nurture their seeds.

The fruit of the Spirit and the gifts of the Spirit are different. Children at different ages require a different approach to parenting. Therefore, godly parents must pay attention to the leading of the Holy Spirit because all our children belong to God. He owns them, owns the earth and its fullness.

Children Represent Fruits And Reward

God's word says, "... the fruit of the womb a reward."

Children represent Fruits because they bring joy to God, their parents and also the world.

John 16:21 says:

> *...A woman giving birth to a child has pain because her time has come, but when her baby is born she forgets the pain because of her joy that a baby is born into the world.*

Children are Fruits because they are meant to be enjoyed by the people around them; the fruits of the spirit they carry in them, are in abundance.

Our children are created in the image of God—just like us—male and female as specified to avoid confusion. God said we should reproduce according to our kind and we reproduced our children, our fruits.

Children as rewards are not limited to just the children you birthed. Every child is the fruit of a womb and a reward or gift. Remember that God, being the owner of all children, can decide through whatever means He wants to use to entrust children into our care and they are all meant to be cherished as rewards or gifts or blessings. Jesus' death took away our sin and grace was made available for all men. It is this grace that qualifies us to parent these children.

Children Represent God's Royal Priesthood

1 Peter 2:9 tells us:

> *... But you are a chosen people, a royal priesthood, a holy nation, God's special possession, that you may declare the praises of him who called you out of darkness into his wonderful light.*

Our children are royalties because they have an identity in God's kingdom and they have royal power through their salvation. Teaching them to meditate and exercise the power in the word of God makes them understand more of their personality in Christ. We ought to enlighten them on the special ministries and gifts of the Holy Spirit and how to work in the power of the Lord.

NOTE: Depending on the age of your children, make it relatable what having an identity in Christ means and how they ought to influence the people around them and the world at large.

Children Represent Happiness, Innocence, And Humility

Psalm 127:5 (KJV) says:

> *Happy is the man that hath his quiver full of them: they shall not be ashamed, but they shall speak with the enemies in the gate.*

When you receive the children God has given you, then you shall be happy. The enemy will not be able to withstand you at the gate. This enemy could represent different challenges of life. Involve your children in the spiritual activities at home, teach them how powerful they are in Christ, and watch what happens when the enemy tries to come near your gates.

Matthew 18:4 (NKJV) says:

> *Therefore whoever humbles himself as this little child is the greatest in the kingdom of heaven.*

In His teachings about the kingdom, Jesus pointed out that the humility and innocence of children are the standards for entering His kingdom. He continued in Matthew 18:6 (NKJV) that:

> *But whoever causes one of these little ones who believe in Me to sin, it would be better for him if a millstone were hung around his neck, and he were drowned in the depth of the sea.*

Take your responsibility for raising them seriously.

Children Represent The Crown To Their Aged Parents

Proverb 17:6 (ESV) says:

Grandchildren are the crown of the aged, and the glory of children is their fathers.

- Children are a crown to their aged parents because they represent honour from God as a royal priesthood.
- Children are a crown to their aged parents because they represent an investment. It is fulfilling to have your children around at your

old age because they remind you of the time, trainings, mouldings, financing, academic, emotions, intercessions and every other form of spiritual and physical investment you made in them.

- Children are a crown to their aged parents because the return on investment parents receive by God's grace is the divine peace and blessing from above when you raise them in the fear of the Lord.

5

Maintaining An Altar Of Prayer As Parents

As believers in Christ, we are operating on the personal covenant we made with God by ourselves, and the existing covenants God made with our fathers in the Bible. This covenant needs to be put alive on the altar of prayer.

This is why it is important to teach your children about God's promises, covenants, blessings, and prophecies of Jesus. Let them not only be familiar with certain scriptures or Bible stories; they ought to chew it into their spirit. Depending on their ages, devise a strategy that could help them memorise certain scriptures. Let them understand that prayer is a compulsory lifestyle of a believer because it takes us to the spiritual realm where we commune with our God.

Acts 6:4 (KJV) says:

But we will give ourselves continually to prayer, and to the ministry of the word

It is our duty as parents to pray for the hearts of our children to be a fertile ground where all the seeds and counsel we sow in them can bear forth fruits (Matthew 13:8).

May the spirit of prayer be in you, as you keep the altar burning, giving life to all covenants.

Teaching The Children About Prayer

Teaching your children about prayer will help them understand that prayer is a communication between them and God.

Give your teenagers more explanations on how this communication channel works; they talk to God and God talks back to them through His word, the small still voice or signs and other means as God desires.

In teaching your children how to talk with God, the believer's standard prayer is found in Matthew 6:1-13 (Our Father who art in heaven…). Teach them how to pray in worship, exalting the name of our God in spiritual songs, psalms, hymns, and in the Holy Ghost if they can understand.

Device a means of teaching your toddlers how prayer time should be. This you can demonstrate by kneeling with two hands clapped together and eyes closed.

You can help by explaining to them why they should thank God for life, food, shelter, toys, their friends, and their grandparents. Use basically things they can relate with.

For your teenagers, teach them how to take turns in family prayers, and other spiritual activities in the house as it suits your family schedule.

Do you still remember this song?

Prayer is the key

Prayer is the key

Prayer is the master key

Jesus started with prayer and ended with prayer

Prayer is the master key.

Interceding For Our Children

God has made us caretakers of His children on earth, it is our duty as parents to intercede on their behalf. Job was a righteous man who hated evil (Job 1:4-5). He had seven sons and three daughters. His sons took turns hosting parties in their homes and invited their sisters.

Job was careful of sin. He made it a habit of assuming his children have offended God after each party and went to God with a burnt offering for each of them, in prayer, to get sanctified.

Embrace the Holy Spirit, our mediator, to help you as you intercede for them and also teach them how to make intercession prayers.

1. As godly parents, we are expected to do some spiritual exercise on behalf of our children as the spirit of God leads us, by:
2. Redeeming them unto God always.
3. Standing on the altar of prayer and waging spiritual wars for them.
4. Giving burnt offerings unto God for their lives.
5. Professing words of deliverance from every evil verdict of the devil.

How To Teach Your Children To Intercede

Intercessory prayer is when your children pray for others, such as their siblings, friends, and other things which may not be a person, like nations, institutions, etc.

In trying to teach your children about intercession, give them a detailed reason why praying for others is a spiritual instruction, which when obeyed, opens us up to spiritual blessings. A good example was Job. The Lord restored the fortunes of Job when he prayed for his friends, and the Lord gave Job twice as much as he had before Job 42:10 AMP. For your toddlers, using a relatable situation like praying on behalf of their sick friend or a family member will help them understand.

For your teenagers, explain the need for them to intercede for their friends, community, schools, churches, orphans, less privileged, and strange acts that are happening around the world like homosexuality, promiscuity, drug addictions, robbery, deadly illness, rape, etc. Make your teens understand that Jesus loves them all, which is why they need to stand in the gap of prayer for their deliverance.

The altar of prayer can give them an encounter with Christ but the responsibility of the parents or guardians is to help God on earth.

The way to draw them to their salvation in Christ is by exposing them to the teachings of Christ. Their encounter with Christ may come in various ways. However, some detailed or documented encounter can spike their hunger for the same.

- Search the scripture for people who have encountered God and what impact it had on their lives.
- Share a family-relatable encounter with God. Depending on the age of your children be creative with your explanation.

- Share your personal encounter with God, if any, or let them read through it if you have them documented.
- Simplify the benefits of having an encounter with God, as such increases their faith in Christ. It gives them a personal conviction without doubt when the situation changes and keeps their spirit life in obedience rather than working in the flesh.
- Explain what quiet time with God means, and share experiences if you have any.
- Assist them on how to begin their prayers, knowing that it is two-way communication.

6

Faith And Solid Foundation In Christ

As godly parents, the number of strongholds that are being projected towards you and your children do not matter before Christ. What is important is your strength and belief in the midst of it all.

God encourages that your faith remains strong, your eyes focused on Christ Jesus, and that you find grace to profess what your spirit sees with your mouth. Also, diligently pray at the altar for deliverance as the case may be and never yield to begging the devil when fear comes knocking at the door. Be confident that He has made you king and prince on earth and you have the keys to the kingdom.

Matthew 16:19 says:

> *I will give you the keys of the kingdom of heaven, and whatever you shall bind on earth shall be bound in heaven, and whatever you shall loose on earth shall be loosed in Heaven.*

Take a look at how the demons begged God in Mark 5:9-13. That incident is enough confidence booster for any godly parent.

In Matthew 13:24-25, Jesus told another parable. He said:

> *The kingdom of heaven is like a man who sowed good seed in his field. But while everyone was sleeping, his enemy came and sowed weeds among the wheat, and went away.*

Children are part of the good seeds we need to sow, nurture and lead into the kingdom of heaven in our small field which is the family. Just as we adults diligently work on our salvation, we need to nurture the children with the teachings of the kingdom, teaching them a reason to store the word of God in their hearts rather than any human-made storage devices that may fail them.

Psalms 119:11 KJV says:

> *Thy word have I hid in mine heart, that I might not sin against thee.*

When we teach them to store the word of God in their hearts, when the enemy comes to sow weeds, our children will be able to sieve through the deception of the enemy because of all we have nurtured in them.

May God strengthen every parent to prayerfully, and watchfully nurture a good seed for God's kingdom, so that the enemy, who is the devil, while we sleep, will not take them away from us in Jesus' name. Amen.

As a godly parent, a lifestyle of testimony can also show how thankful we are to God for His wondrous works (Psalms 71:15-18). Involve the children in the Lord's doings, teach and explain to them what the Lord has been doing in their lives, in the home, and in the lives of people around them. Also, using scripture-based Jesus stories helps to build their belief and trust in God.

As a godly parent, you may want to document your family testimonies to fall back on them with your children as Jesus tarries.

Jesus was going around doing good, teaching while speaking in parables (Mark 4:1-20, 1 Corinthians 3:6-9).

Remember this:

The Seed —Your Teachings

The Soil — Children's Heart

The Farmer — The Parents

The Plant — Children

Increaser — God

How do we prepare their heart before planting the seeds?

- Present unto God your seeds (Teachings) in prayers. From the day the Son of Man was lifted from the earth, He drew all men to himself. Our effort as parents are needed but God works in the heart of our children.
- Embrace divine wisdom from the written word of God. Do not contradict the word of God.
- Work hand in hand with the Holy Spirit. The function of the Holy Spirit can never be overemphasised. In planting seeds (Teachings) that will grow on good soil (Heart), we need The Spirit to teach us all things. He spots our weaknesses in the planting process. The Holy Spirit prepares and equips you ahead for the challenges the plant (children) will face as they sprout out.
- 1 Corinthians 3:6-9 says: I planted the seed, Apollos watered it, but God has been making it grow. So neither the one who plants nor the one who waters is anything, but only God, who makes things grow. The one who plants and the one who waters have one purpose, and they will each be rewarded according to their own labor. For we are co-workers in God's service; you are God's field, God's building.

What Is The State Of Your Health And That Of Your Children?

As godly parents, focus less on negative reports around the world. Nevertheless, don't be ignorant of the devices of the enemy in the world you live in. The ability to balance your mind between fear and faith will be evident in what you pass on to your children. During these challenging times, the children are watching their parents' reactions to this whole situation.

After taking advice from medical practitioners, it is also of great importance that you take some spiritual supplements to boost your children's immune system.

Joshua 1:8 (KJV) says:

> *This book of the law shall not depart out of thy mouth; but thou shalt meditate therein day and night, that thou mayest observe to do according to all that is written therein: for then thou shalt make thy way prosperous, and then thou shall have good success.*

When faced with stormy seasons of life, stay strong, maintain the connection with God and chew His word to draw inner peace.

Isaiah 41:10 tells us:

> *So do not fear, for I am with you; do not be dismayed, for I am your God. I will strengthen you and help you; I will uphold you with my righteous right hand.*

The storms of life come to steal your peace, health, finance, joy, and other things. As godly parents, the state of your heart, mind, mental health, emotions, physical strength and more are all needed for the parenting responsibilities that await us this year and more years to come.

In John 16:33 we read:

> *I have told you these things, so that in me you may have peace. In this world, you will have trouble. But take heart! I have overcome the world.*

May our children not lack the care they need from us when we are faced with storms of life. AMEN.

7

Discipleship With Our Children

Discipleship can be understood and practised in different ways. Today our concern is how a godly parent should embrace discipleship with her children. Discipleship is a spiritual act of fellowship with our children. Knowing that God himself is present among His people makes it an extraordinary gathering. Discipling our children gives both the godly parent and the children grace to grow spiritually. Deut 6:4-7.

How To Disciple Your Children

As a godly parent have a set time or suitable time for fellowship/discipleship where explaining things and giving the children the opportunity to ask questions is encouraged.

You don't have to be a Bible expert to disciple your children. The Bible is your instructional manual. As a parent, create a deep hunger for the work of the Holy Spirit. Most times, the kind of questions children ask may take you unaware. It takes divine wisdom and deep insight from the Holy Spirit to answer their questions and make them understand.

Ephesians 1:17 says:

> *I keep asking that the God of our Lord Jesus Christ, the glorious Father, may give you the Spirit of wisdom and revelation, so that you may know him better.*

The study of the word of God is a vital tool to making discipleship profitable to you and your children as He unfolds mysteries to you all, gives insight, and strengthens everyone's spirituality.

Discipling also prepares our children for profitable kingdom services like evangelising, standing on the truth of God's word, and giving them an idea of how to personally work out their salvation for the race ahead.

Evangelism Is Every Believer's Duty Likewise The Parents And Children

FOCUS: Toddlers and Pre-teenagers

Evangelism is a must for every believer (speaking about Jesus and his good works), and not a Christian responsibility meant only for an evangelist.

In trying to catch them young, godly parents need to teach their children the need to win souls for Christ. According to the Bible, whoever does so is wise. As godly parents, we need to encourage our children to partake in spiritual activities, because obeying them attracts spiritual blessings; the children without knowing are investing in their future.

1 Peter 3:15 says:

But in your hearts revere Christ as Lord. Always be prepared to give an answer to everyone who asks you to give the reason for the hope that you have. But do this with gentleness and respect.

How To Guide The Toddlers

Power In The Name Of Jesus: Teach them that using these powerful lines of words "JESUS LOVES YOU" and "IN THE NAME OF JESUS" can calm a wounded heart.

In Acts 2:38 we read that:

Peter replied, "Repent and be baptized, every one of you, in the name of Jesus Christ for the forgiveness of your sins. And you will receive the gift of the Holy Spirit.

Christ-Like Lifestyle: Teach them how to obey commandments and morals while with their friends, such as taking a stand not to lie, compromise, or bear false witness against their classmates, friends, and siblings. In doing so, they reflect the image of Christ and identify with Him; this speaks more to the people around them (Matthew 10:33).

2 Cor 5:20 says:

> *We are therefore Christ's ambassadors, as though God were making his appeal through us. We implore you on Christ's behalf: Be reconciled to God.*

Prayer: Teach them how to use prayer to draw souls unto God. They may be concerned about someone's way of life. Make them understand that standing in prayer for the person can invite God to step into the situation. God needs more labourers.

In Matthew 9:37-38, we read what Jesus said:

> *Then he said to his disciples, "The harvest is plentiful but the workers are few. Ask the Lord of the harvest, therefore, to send out workers into his harvest field."*

Organised Evangelism: Allow your children to be involved in family evangelism. Allow them to accompany you to organised Christian evangelism and remember to have their comfort at heart through the process. Let them do the basics of sharing tracks and other Godly-related materials.

Mark 16:15 commanded us to:

> *... Go into all the world and preach the gospel to all creation.*

Tips On Teens Evangelism

Teenagers may question their parents about why they have to evangelise. Raising godly teenagers is a greater responsibility. All godly parents must be open to unexpected questions and reactions from their teens. The Holy Spirit is the companion that godly parents need to guide their teens.

Also, desiring to have the gift of the Holy Spirit (discernment) will help parents through different encounters with their teens. Again, scriptural explanation while explaining spiritual matters to them is key.

How A Teenager Can Evangelise

Godly Advice: A teenager to an extent understands what is good and bad. In their dealings among their peers, teach them how to give good counsel wherever they find themselves.

Choice of Expression: This could be:

a. Verbal Expression: Teach them how to consciously filter their words in their day-to-day communication, letting them know, that they carry the presence of God everywhere they go as believers.

b. Body Language Expression: Teach them how teens who have identified themselves in Jesus Christ need to carry their bodies as the temple of the Holy Spirit. They need not make unholy gestures or signals to the public with their body language.

Social Media: As a godly parent, carefully devise a means to let your teenagers understand that whatever identity they build on social media, goes a long way in showing if they are for or against Christ. Make them understand that social media is a platform where they have control and an opportunity to influence their generation with godly vibes.

Social Gathering: As godly parents, it is our responsibility to help our teenagers understand the need to have fun in a godly manner. Let them have this question in their mind — if Jesus were here, what would He do? — knowing that Jesus is our role model. Teach them how to shine God's light and be salt to the world.

School Environment: As a godly parent, before your teenagers get into higher institutions, try to understand what life looks like in such an environment. Prepare them on time for living alone and being sold out to Christ so that all their friends, coursemates, and roommates will know that they live for Christ (lifestyle).

Divine Power: Teach them how the power of God working in their lives can bring souls to the Lord's feet. Teach them not to act religious but embrace the power that makes them religious.2 Tim 3:5 tell us how people in the last days will be lost playing religion but denying the power of Christ whom they confess. May our children not deny the power of Christ in them.

8

Training The Children To Serve God And Humanity

As godly parents, we need to teach our children ways to serve God and humanity, not as a burden but as a privilege. Our children should be made to understand the kingdom instructions in God's word, which is for their own profit.

2 Timothy 3:16 (AMP) says:

> *All Scripture is God-breathed [given by divine inspiration] and is profitable for instruction, for conviction [of sin], for correction [of error and restoration to obedience], for training in righteousness [learning to live in conformity to God's will, both publicly and privately-behaving honorably with personal integrity and moral courage]*

Make them understand that their motive for doing anything should be pure (knowing that God searches our hearts and weighs our motives according to

Proverb 21:2) and not boastful. They shouldn't compete for or manipulate one another but they should obey the commandments of God and show love, which is the greatest commandment of all.

Proverbs 22:6 (KJV) says:

> *Train up a child in the way he should go: and when he is old, he will not depart from it.*

Here are some ways to train your children:

- Make the things of God a priority in your home from when your children are young.
- Guard your emotional health. Refuse negative attitudes/words when your heart is worried. Romans 12:2 says:
  Do not conform to the pattern of this world, but be transformed by the renewing of your mind. Then you will be able to test and approve what God's will is—his good, pleasing and perfect will.
- Supplement their faith in God with moral excellence because they are the salt and light of this world.
- The family experiences and training they undergo shape their thinking process.

Teaching Your Children To Glorify God And Bless Men With Their Gifts

James 1:17 (NIV) says:

> *Every good and perfect gift is from above, coming down from the Father of the heavenly lights, who does not change like shifting shadows.*

1 Peter 4:10 (NIV) says:

> *Each of you should use whatever gift you have received to serve others, as faithful stewards of God's grace in its various forms.*

As godly parents, we have the privilege to nurture our children's gifts—both natural, spiritual, and trained gifts. God the giver of good gifts expects our children to use their gifts to bless humanity and to glorify Him as the giver. Our duty as godly parents is to teach them how to do this.

- Teach them to have a fruitful kingdom motive in using their gift to win souls and be a blessing on earth.
- Proverb 16:2 says:
  All a person's ways seem pure to them but motives are weighed by the Lord.

- Teach them how to faithfully seek divine wisdom and direction from the giver of good gifts (Job 28:12-18).
- Teach them how to lean on God's word for inspiration, creativity, impartation, ideas, and finance.
  Matthew 6:33 says:
  But seek first his kingdom and his righteousness, and all these things will be given to you as well.)

Raising Children As Leaders For The Future

Godly parenting requires a form of leadership from every parent. Our parenting leadership involves maximising our given talents, strength, acts of service, acquired skills gotten as a result of being a parent, or learned skills.

In 1 Peter 4:10, we read that:

> *Each of you should use whatever gift you have received to serve others, as faithful stewards of God's grace in its various forms.*

One of the important roles of our leadership towards the children is being able to serve them, nurture their potential or personalities, and lead them well.

Samson's parents tried to understand their leadership roles. They also involved their son's creator who holds the manual for raising godly children. They inquired on the altar of prayer for God's will and guidance.

Raising Available Children For The Lord's Use

As a godly parent (married or single parenting), God is searching for faithful men for His own use. He is relying on us to train, mould, and sharpen our children for His use. Psalm 78:5-6 says:

> *He decreed statutes for Jacob and established the law in Israel, which he commanded our ancestors to teach their children, so the next generation would know them, even the children yet to be born, and they in turn would tell their children.*

We aren't meant to wait until our children are grown before we start preparing them for the master's use. Every child has a divine mandate; it does not matter if the child grows up to have the title of pastor or not. We are all vessels in God's hands.

In Ezekiel 22:30, this played out:

> *I looked for someone among them who would build up the wall and stand before me in the gap*

on behalf of the land so I would not have to destroy it, but I found no one.

The parents of that time in the scripture above could not raise faithful men because God found no one to use. May we not disappoint God in raising our children. Amen!

The world is after the minds of children, so it's our responsibility to do the following:

- Saturate their minds with God's word.
  Psalm 119:105 says:
  Thy word is a lamp unto my feet and light unto my Path.
- Speak good prophecies into their lives.
- Be sensitive to their day-to-day living.
- Engage them in spiritual activities just the same way they are active in schools e.g. Bible reading and stories, singing, church activities, evangelism, and visits to orphanages and hospitals.
- Ask or carefully watch who your children idolise in their hearts as role models. Let Jesus be their example while you be their closest earthly role model by living a Christlike life.
- Family as an institution ordained by God stands as a structure for society. Various leadership positions in the world are occupied by people who were once children, raised or shaped with

different family values. Today God is asking you, what type of children are you raising for His end-times agenda?

As godly parents, God is dependent on us to raise godly children who will represent and honour Him with their different leadership positions in the world. I hear Him asking if we can raise better children who can be or be better like the following:

- **Daniel**: He was a scholar and a politician among other things, and he held on to God's truth (Daniel 5:11-12).
- **Timothy:** He was a Bishop, full of faith in God (2nd Timothy 1:1-5).
- **Job**: He was an influential businessman yet righteous. He feared God and hated evil (Job 1:1-3).

Adopting And Fostering A Child

Most times, divine love demands certain responsibility from us. Fostering and Adoption are areas many Christians neglect.

The scripture has shown us how deeply Jesus loves the little children. So, if you have chosen to please God, shouldn't you also do that which pleases Him if you can?

Certain responsibilities require a lot more commitment than others, but when we make our plans, the Lord sets them for us.

Key Takeaway

1. Take a child out of the street.
2. Be a Godly parent to an orphan.
3. Being able to have your own children, is not an excuse.
4. Be convinced that you are graced to take up such responsibility, mentally and otherwise.
5. Shelter the less privileged children.
6. Be led divinely for such responsibilities.
7. Understand the legal requirements involved.

Make a sacrifice; you will not regret it.

If Pharaoh's daughter, in Exodus 2:1-10, could foster baby Moses, then you by God's grace can do more.

9
Parental Lessons

It pleases God to use us to bring children into this earth, but a lot of times, we fail Him. We fail Him when we lose contact with Him. We fail Him when we disconnect in communicating and partnering with Him to raise the fruits He has given to us. We fail Him when we allow society and peer groups to decide what direction our children should take rather than ask the creator himself.

Here are some lessons we can learn to inspire us in this direction.

Lessons From Samson's Birth

- Samson's birth was significant because he was to deliver Israel out of the hands of the Philistines. Every child we have received from the Lord is called to be a solution provider.
- Samson's parents knew and feared their God. They knew the right spirit to believe when a message came to them.

- Samson's parents inquired on the altar of prayer for God's will and guidance. It only takes faith and one who hunger and understands the value of God's will to lay at the altar like Samson's mother did for a child whom she had not even 'conceived', asking the Lord to send back the angel who will teach them on how to raise Samson when he was born. His parents were in the era when God's children hadn't received the Holy Spirit but had to wait for Angels or the voice of the Lord to speak to them. Today, we have the Holy Spirit who teaches us "ALL THINGS." But the question is, do we inquire of the Lord how He wants us to train our children to meet up to His will (part of which is being a solution provider to their generation)?
- Samson's parents obeyed spiritual instructions on behalf of their unborn baby (Judges13:14).

There are blessings attached to obeying spiritual instructions concerning our children and unborn babies. Samson's mother acknowledged she was to dedicate the child to God. She knew she was only a vessel to bring the child into the world. This shows that parents should dedicate their children even before they are born.

Samson's parents gave sacrifice and thanks to God concerning their son even before he was "conceived " in the womb. This act of faith and thanksgiving should be a habitual thing in the life of every parent. We should declare the promises of God over our children and believe they will be established. Samson was born and the spirit of the Lord began to use him. God's word does not return to Him void until it has accomplished the purpose for which it was sent. Be patient!

May we receive God's grace as we partner more with the Almighty in our parenting. Amen.

Lesson From Jesus' Death

After Jesus was conceived, His parents began to make inquiries from God on how to embark on the leadership role of training a godly seed on earth as well as nurturing His potential for effective ministry.

Psalm 144:12 says:

> *Then our sons in their youth will be like well-nurtured plants, and our daughters will be like pillars carved to adorn a palace.*

Part of His leadership role was to serve us through death; washing away our sins. His death was not just a service and sacrifice, there are lessons for us to learn.

- Jesus' journey to the cross teaches us how to pray in accordance with God's will. As godly parents, when we are faced with some parenting challenges, we should pray for God's will just like Jesus did in Matthew 26:37-39.

- Jesus' journey to the cross birthed the promise of the Holy Spirit, who teaches us all things, including God's divine manual for godly parenting (John 14:26, John 15:26-27, John 14;16, John 16:17).
- Jesus' journey to the cross took away every parenting fear, mistake, guilt, shame, faulty foundation, and sin (John 1:29, 1 John 3:5).
- Jesus' journey to the cross gave us room to desire the gifts of the Holy Spirit that makes our parenting responsibility easier and panic-free (I Cor 12: 1-end).
- Jesus in all His suffering while on the journey to His death teaches every godly parent how to hold peace as He did in Matthew 26:63.
- Jesus' journey to the cross teaches us service as godly parents (John 13:1-17).

A Quick Check-Up For Every Godly Parent

1. Are you preparing the road to salvation early? Ephesians 2:8-10
2. Are you still prioritising God's interest in your home? Matthew 6:33
3. Have you been teaching your children the word of God? Deuteronomy 6:6-7
4. Are you tired of standing in the gap of prayers for them? Thessalonians 5:16-18
5. Are you still on duty as the earthly parent, receiving instructions from God on how to lead the children you received from Him?
6. Does your lifestyle reflect Christ before them?
7. How evident is your garment of Love, Thanksgiving, Faith, Giving, Salvation, and Obedience to God's word?
8. How often do you remind your children of God's blessings, covenant, promises, prophecies, and the gifts of the Holy Spirit?

Acknowledgements

I sincerely appreciate God for the grace and inspiration to write this book.

I thank my parents for nurturing me into what I have become today with the help of God.

I also thank my husband and children for all their sacrifices and support. God bless you all.